MORLEY LIBRARY
3 0112 1057 8707 8

# Communication
## Past and Present

by Kerry Dinmont

BUMBA BOOKS™

LERNER PUBLICATIONS ◆ MINNEAPOLIS

**Note to Educators:**

Throughout this book, you'll find critical thinking questions. These can be used to engage young readers in thinking critically about the topic and in using the text and photos to do so.

Copyright © 2019 by Lerner Publishing Group, Inc.

All rights reserved. International copyright secured. No part of this book may be reproduced, stored in a retrieval system, or transmitted in any form or by any means—electronic, mechanical, photocopying, recording, or otherwise—without the prior written permission of Lerner Publishing Group, Inc., except for the inclusion of brief quotations in an acknowledged review.

Lerner Publications Company
A division of Lerner Publishing Group, Inc.
241 First Avenue North
Minneapolis, MN 55401 USA

For reading levels and more information, look up this title at www.lernerbooks.com.

**Library of Congress Cataloging-in-Publication Data**

Names: Dinmont, Kerry, 1982– author.
Title: Communication past and present / Kerry Dinmont.
Description: Minneapolis : Lerner Publications, [2018] | Series: Bumba books — past and present | Includes bibliographical references and index.
Identifiers: LCCN 2017058728 (print) | LCCN 2018001186 (ebook) | ISBN 9781541507753 (eb pdf) | ISBN 9781541503311 (hardcover) | ISBN 9781541526877 (softcover)
Subjects:  LCSH: Communication—History—Juvenile literature.
Classification: LCC P91.2 (ebook) | LCC P91.2 .D34 2018 (print) | DDC 302.2/09—dc23

LC record available at https://lccn.loc.gov/2017058728

Manufactured in the United States of America
1 – CG – 7/15/18

# Table of Contents

Communication through History 4

Then and Now 22

Picture Glossary 23

Read More 24

Index 24

# Communication through History

There are many ways to communicate.

Communication was different in

the past.

Long ago, people often wrote letters.

Mail carriers delivered them on foot.

People still sometimes mail letters.

But trucks make delivery faster.

What else might make mail delivery faster now?

The telegraph was invented in the 1800s.

This machine sent messages.

Machines still send messages. But they look different from a telegraph.

**What kinds of machines send messages now?**

People used to use radio waves to talk from far away.

People can still talk using radio waves.

Radios also play music.

But many people talk and play music on their phones.

People used phones long ago too.

But all phones had cords and wires.

**How else do you think phones long ago were different?**

How do you communicate?

20

# Then and Now

## Then

Mail was delivered on foot.

Telegraphs sent messages.

Radio waves were used to talk from far away.

## Today

Mail is delivered by truck.

Computers send messages.

Cell phones let us talk from far away.

22

# Picture Glossary

**communicate**: to share ideas or words

**delivered**: taken to someone

**radio waves**: waves that move through the air and that carry sounds

**telegraph**: a machine that sends messages over a wire

# Read More

Abramovitz, Melissa. *How Do Computers Talk to One Another?* Minneapolis: Lerner Publications, 2016.

Boothroyd, Jennifer. *From Chalkboards to Computers: How Schools Have Changed.* Minneapolis: Lerner Publications, 2012.

Zuchora-Walske, Christine. *What's Inside My Computer?* Minneapolis: Lerner Publications, 2016.

# Index

machines, 11–12

mail carriers, 7

music, 16

phones, 16, 18

radio waves, 15–16

telegraph, 11–12

## Photo Credits

The images in this book are used with the permission of: © wavebreakmedia/Shutterstock.com, p. 5; © Everett Historical/Shutterstock.com, pp. 6–7, 23 (top right); © Monkey Business Images/Shutterstock.com, p. 9; © villorejo/Shutterstock.com, pp. 10, 23 (bottom right); © bbernard/Shutterstock.com, p. 13; © Everett Collection/Shutterstock.com, p. 14; © Ronnachai Palas/Shutterstock.com, p. 17; © Trairong Praditsan/Shutterstock.com, pp. 18–19; © kali9/iStock.com, pp. 20–21; © sirtravelalot/Shutterstock.com, p. 22; © 9george/Shutterstock.com, p. 23 (top left); © matka_Wariatka/Shutterstock.com, p. 23 (bottom left).

Front Cover: © Devonyu/iStock.com, left; © scanrail/iStock.com, right.